How to Attract Attention in the Animal World

LOOK
AT ME!

STEVE JENKINS AND ROBIN PAGE

Houghton Mifflin Harcourt   Boston   New York

Most of the time, animals do their best to blend in with their surroundings. A predator that is easy to spot can frighten away its prey. And, of course, staying hidden is a good idea for any animal that risks becoming a meal for another creature.

But sometimes an animal *wants* to stand out. Perhaps it's signaling a mate or warning a predator that it is poisonous. It might be defending its territory or trying to lure its prey.

Some animals attract attention by being noisy or smelly. But visual display—flashing a bright color, performing a dance, glowing in the dark, even blowing up like a balloon—is the most common way an animal says, "Look at me!"

Look at my big red balloon!

How does a male **hooded seal** attract a mate and warn other males to stay away? He fills a hood on top of his head with air. He also inflates a sack of skin hanging from his nose and shakes it back and forth.

The **magnificent frigatebird** spends most of its life in the air, rarely landing. It even sleeps on the wing. But when it's time to start a family, a male frigatebird finds a spot on the ground and signals a female by inflating a bright red pouch of skin on his throat.

Watch me grow—and grow.

As it lies motionless on a branch, the **twig snake** looks like part of the tree. But if it is threatened, the snake puffs up its throat. This makes it look bigger and scarier.

The **great horned owl** reacts to a threat by spreading its wings and pointing them downward. Now the owl looks larger and more intimidating.

When it inflates itself with water, the **pufferfish** isn't easy to swallow. Swelling up also causes its sharp spines to point outward, making the puffer an unappealing meal for a bigger fish.

The **common toad** blends in with the leaves and grass of its habitat. But if it can't hide, it takes a deep breath and blows itself up like a football. Now a predator might decide that the toad is too big to swallow.

All dressed up.

Every summer, a colorful plume of feathers appears around the neck of the **great crested grebe**. Male and female grebes show off this decoration during their mating dance.

The brilliant feathered crest of the **royal flycatcher** usually lies flat against its head. But when it's time to find a mate, both male and female birds raise their colorful headdresses to say, "Here I am!"

Shall we dance?

The **Mediterranean mantis** responds to danger by striking a threatening pose, swaying from side to side, and revealing large eyespots on its wings. This performance can startle a predator.

The male **blue-spotted mudskipper** impresses a female by raising its fins and leaping into the air. This display also warns other males to stay away.

It takes two.

To get a female's attention, the male **blue-footed booby** performs an elaborate mating dance. If she seems interested, he stomps his feet to show off their bright blue color.

Male and female **Japanese cranes** partner in a graceful duet. The birds are getting to know each other, something that will help them work together to build a nest and raise their chicks.

Stand back!

The venomous **scorpion** curls its tail over its back as a warning—it is ready to strike. The stinger on the tip of its tail can inject a deadly toxin.

The male **fiddler crab** waves his colorful, oversize claw. He uses the claw as a weapon in fights with other males over territory or mates.

Mandrills live in groups, called troops, which may include hundreds of monkeys. Males that rule their troop develop intensely colorful faces. This mandrill senses a threat and makes a warning face.

Look what I can do!

When the **Budgett's frog** is in danger, it inflates its body, stands on tiptoe, and screams loudly. This frog has teeth, and it will lunge and try to bite an attacker.

An alarmed **springbok** leaps straight up, bounding high above the ground. This performance is called "pronking," and it tells lions and other predators, "I'm healthy, and I'm too fast to catch."

A male **hippopotamus** is serious about protecting its territory. It cautions other males to stay away by opening its mouth and displaying its long tusks.

A brilliant warning.

There are thousands of species of **sea slug**. Most of them are poisonous, and their bright colors are a warning. They let predators know that eating a sea slug would be a mistake.

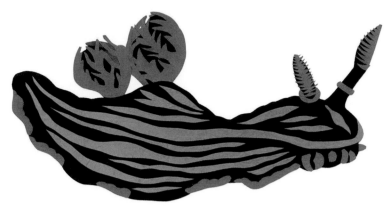

variable neon slug

Willan's chromodoris *(kro-mo-door-is)*

streaked chromodoris

regal sea goddess

opalescent nudibranch *(new-dih-branch)*

Colorful **poison dart frogs** are easy to spot among the green foliage of their rainforest home. The skin of these little frogs contains a powerful toxin, and their vivid hues warn their enemies to leave them alone.

golden poison dart frog

strawberry poison dart frog

blue poison dart frog

green and black poison dart frog

phantasmal poison dart frog

Dressed to impress.

The intense colors of the **mandarinfish** help it attract a mate. They are also a warning: the skin of this fish oozes toxic mucus.

The feathers of the male **mandarin duck** are usually dull gray and brown. During mating season, however, the male's plumage is transformed into an array of brilliant colors.

To impress a female, a male **red bird of paradise** performs an acrobatic courtship ritual high in the branches of a tree.

Take a look at this!

Male **Carolina anoles** have a pink or orange throat pouch, called a dewlap. They extend this flap of skin to get the attention of a female and warn other males to stay away.

The male **Indian bullfrog** is normally a dull green color. But when it's time to look for a mate, his body turns bright yellow and he inflates two large blue sacs of skin on his neck.

Surprise!

The bright colors of the **common milkweed locust** announce that this insect is poisonous. Its body secretes a toxic foam as a defense against predators. And when it spreads its wings, the sudden flash of red that appears can startle an attacker.

The **sarcastic fringehead** fiercely protects its territory. If another fish approaches, it opens its huge mouth and reveals rows of sharp teeth. If that doesn't frighten away an intruder, the sarcastic fringehead will lunge and try to bite.

Got a light?

*Photuris (**faht-ur-is**)* is a kind of **firefly**, a beetle that can glow in the dark. The female *Photuris* imitates the mating flashes of other species of firefly. These flashes attract a male, who thinks he's found a partner. When he shows up, however, the *Photuris* female devours him.

The bioluminescent **deep-sea dragonfish** produces its own light. Its glowing barbel—the long, fleshy tentacle that emerges from its jaw—is a lure that attracts smaller fish to their doom.

You've been warned.

When frightened, the **regal ringneck snake** releases a smelly liquid, rolls onto its back, and plays dead. Its colorful belly warns predators that this snake tastes terrible.

The **hooded pitohui** is one of the world's few poisonous birds— its skin and flesh contain potent toxins. The bird's bright orange feathers warn potential predators to stay away.

Ladybird beetles, or ladybugs, are poisonous and taste terrible, so most animals won't eat them. The **ladybird mimic spider** fools hungry birds by imitating the appearance of a ladybug.

Look—over here!

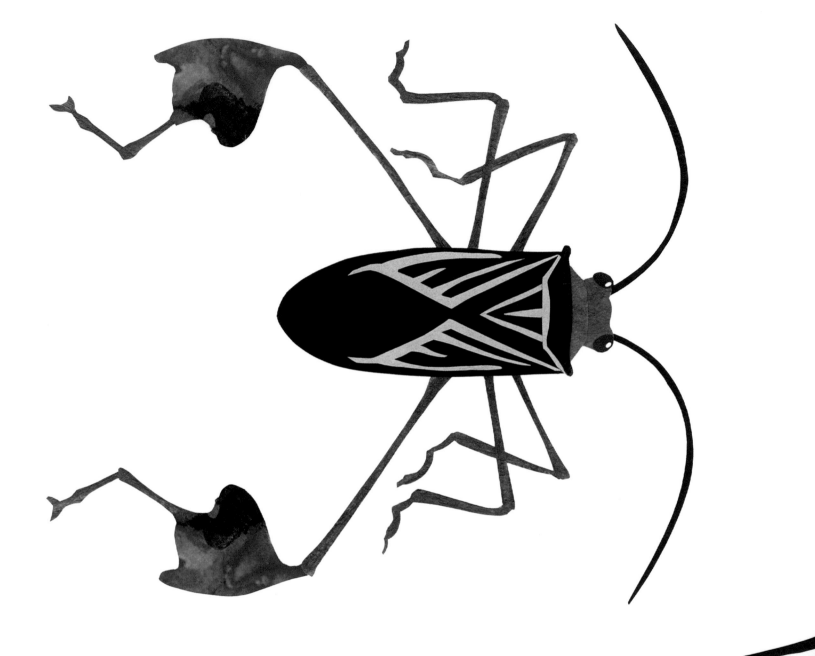

The **flag-footed bug** flutters its legs to distract a predator. An attacker will often go after the bug's leaflike foot instead of its body.

The male **long-tailed widowbird** puts on an aerial display to charm a female. He cruises back and forth just above the ground, trailing his long tail feathers behind him.

Here's looking at you.

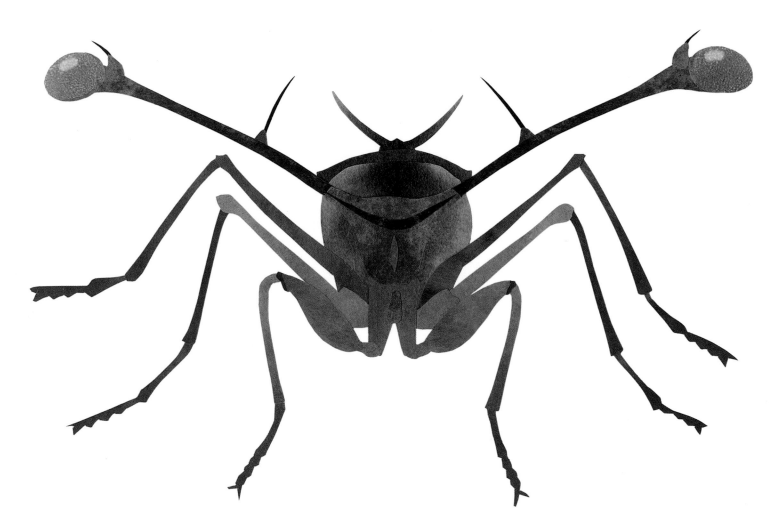

Soon after taking on its adult form, the **stalk-eyed fly** pumps air into its eyestalks, which grow longer and longer. Female stalk-eyed flies prefer mates that have the longest eyestalks.

The **big skate** glides
along the sea floor.
When it is seen from
above, its two large
fake eyes, or eyespots,
can frighten away
a shark or other
predator.

More eyespots!

With its wings folded, the **bullseye moth** looks like a dead leaf. But if it is disturbed, it spreads its wings and reveals a startling splash of color and two large eyespots.

The **four-eyed butterflyfish** has two real eyes and two fake ones. The eyespots trick predators into attacking the wrong end of the fish.

This is the end...

The male **ring-tailed lemur** waves his tail in the air to attract a female. He also uses his tail in "stink fights" with other males. The lemur has scent glands on his shoulders and wrists. He rubs this scent onto his tail, then shakes it at another male.

Why are the males of many species so colorful?

It's a fact: the males of many animal species are much more flamboyant than the females. They often display bright colors or elaborate body parts to attract a mate or warn off other males. At first, this may not seem fair—why shouldn't females be just as colorful?

But this arrangement makes sense. When a male displays bright colors or does an elaborate dance, he is letting a female know that he is strong and healthy and will make a good father for her babies. But this kind of display has a cost—it puts him at greater risk of being spotted and killed by a predator. The female, soon to be a mother, needs to stay alive to provide for her babies. She plays it smart—her less colorful skin, fur, or feathers blend in with her environment and help to keep her safe.

A male **hooded seal** can reach eight feet (2½ meters) in length. These seals live on floating ice in the frigid waters of the North Atlantic and Arctic Oceans. They prey on shrimp, fish, and shellfish. Their nose sack and hood are used for display and for making sounds that can attract or warn off other seals.

The **magnificent frigatebird** soars above the warm coastal waters of the North and South American coasts. It is a large bird, with an eight-foot (2½-meter) wingspan. Its diet includes fish, squid, jellyfish, and other small animals that it scoops up from the water's surface.

The **twig snake** lives in the forests of central and southern Africa. It gets its name from its habit of swaying gently, imitating the motion of a twig in the wind. It spends its entire life in the trees, where it hunts frogs, lizards, other snakes, and birds. Twig snakes reach five feet (1½ meters) in length. They are venomous, and their bite has caused human deaths.

The **great horned owl** is nocturnal—it is active at night. This owl is a large, powerful hunter, with a wingspan of up to five feet (1½ meters). It preys on rabbits, snakes, and other birds, as well as smaller animals such as mice and frogs. Great horned owls inhabit much of North and Central America. They are also found in the temperate parts of South America.

There are many different species of **pufferfish.** The smallest is only one inch (2½ centimeters) long, while the largest can reach 39 inches (1 meter) in length. With the exception of the cold polar seas, pufferfish inhabit all of the world's oceans. They eat smaller fish, algae, shrimp, and crabs. The flesh of this fish contains one of the strongest poisons in the animal world. One pufferfish can contain enough toxins to kill thirty adult humans.

The **common toad** is found throughout most of Europe as well as parts of western Asia and North Africa. It is about seven inches (18 centimeters) long, and it feeds on insects, worms, and spiders. This toad can alter the color of its skin to blend in with its surroundings. If hiding doesn't work, it stands up tall and inflates itself with air. This makes the toad look larger, and warns predators that its skin contains a deadly toxin.

During the summer, the **great crested grebe** lives on ponds and lakes in the warm parts of Europe and Asia. In the winter it migrates to Africa, India, and Australia. Grebes are large birds, reaching 20 inches (51 centimeters) in length. They are good swimmers and divers, and they hunt fish, insects, and other small water-dwelling animals.

Male and female **royal flycatchers** signal each other by swaying side-to-side with their feathered fans held erect. These birds live in the forests of Central and South America. They are about seven inches (18 centimeters) long, and they feed on flying insects.

The **Mediterranean mantis,** native to southern Europe and the Middle East, has also been introduced to parts of Asia and North America. This fierce predatory insect is about two and a half inches (6½ centimeters) long. It is an ambush hunter. It waits quietly, then lunges to grab bees, grasshoppers, butterflies, and other insects with its spiked legs.

The **blue-spotted mudskipper** can breathe through its skin as well as through its gills. This allows it to leave the water to escape danger or search for food. These fish, which grow up to 12 inches (30 centimeters) long, are often found among the roots of mangrove trees in Southeast Asia. They eat water plants and small aquatic animals.

The **blue-footed booby** lives along the warm Pacific coasts of Central and South America. The blue color of its feet comes from pigments in the fish it eats. Bright blue feet indicate a healthy bird, and females favor the males with the most intensely colored feet. Blue-footed boobies are large birds, with a wingspan reaching five feet (1½ meters).

The **Japanese crane,** also known as the red-crowned crane, lives in China, northeastern Russia, and northern Japan. It nests near rivers and wetlands, and feeds on fish, frogs, lizards, snails, and insects. It also eats rice and other grains. These elegant birds stand more than five feet (1½ meters) tall, with a wingspan of eight feet (2½ meters).

There are more than 1,700 different kinds of **scorpion.** They are found almost everywhere in the world except for the polar regions. The smallest scorpion is no larger than a housefly, while the largest reaches nine inches (23 centimeters) in length. Scorpions are predators. They paralyze their prey—insects, spiders, lizards, and small rodents—with their venomous sting. About 25 kinds of scorpion are deadly to humans. The most dangerous of all is the

fat-tailed scorpion, which is responsible for about five thousand human deaths every year.

Fiddler crabs excavate burrows on the sandy beaches and muddy tidal flats of warm seacoasts around the world. They are small crabs—the largest is only about two inches (5 centimeters) across. They sift through sand and mud to pick out bits of algae, microscopic creatures, and pieces of decaying plants or animals.

The **mandrill** inhabits the tropical rainforests of West Africa. It grazes on plant stems, fruit, and leaves, but also consumes insects, eggs, frogs, and rodents. Weighing as much as 80 pounds (36 kilograms), it is big enough to kill and eat an antelope or other small grazing animals. If another monkey pushes the dominant male out of his leadership role, his colorful facial markings will slowly fade.

The **Budgett's frog** lives in southeastern South America, where it hunts insects, snails, and other frogs. It is about five inches (12½ centimeters) long. In the dry season, it burrows into the mud and wraps itself in multiple layers of skin to keep from drying out.

The **springbok,** a kind of antelope, lives in southern Africa where it grazes on grass and shrubs. Because it obtains the water it needs from the plants it eats, a springbok can go its entire life

without taking a drink. This small antelope stands about 30 inches (76 centimeters) at the shoulder. It is one of the fastest animals in Africa. Among predators, only the cheetah is faster. Lions and leopards rarely even try to catch it.

The **hippopotamus** is one of the most dangerous large animals in Africa. The hippo weighs as much as 3,300 pounds (1,500 kilograms), and it is responsible for hundreds of human deaths every year. Hippos eat leaves and grass, feeding mostly at night and spending the hot days submerged in rivers and lakes. To prevent sunburn, hippos secrete a reddish natural sunscreen. This has led to the myth that hippos sweat blood.

Sea slugs are found in all the world's warm and tropical oceans. They range from one-fourth inch (6 millimeters) to 12 inches (30 centimeters) in length. Many sea slugs are highly toxic and live near colorful coral reefs. Their intense colors and patterns serve as both warning and camouflage. Most nudibranchs—the kind of sea slugs shown here—are carnivores. They eat shellfish, other sea slugs, and sponges.

The toxin of the **golden poison dart frog** is the most potent of any animal on earth. It is just two inches (5 centimeters) long, but its skin contains enough poison to kill ten adult humans. There are more than a hundred different kinds of poison dart frog living in the jungles of Central and South America. Many of them are dangerous to touch, but some people keep them as pets. In the wild, these frogs get their toxins from the insects they eat. If they are fed nontoxic food, they are not poisonous and are safe to handle.

 Mandarinfish live in the warm waters of the western Pacific Ocean and grow to about three inches (7½ centimeters) in length. They use their fins to walk along the sea floor, hunting shrimp, worms, and other small animals.

 The male **mandarin duck** may be the world's most colorful bird, at least when it is wearing its "look at me" plumage. These birds are native to Japan, Korea, eastern Russia, and China. They are about 18 inches (46 centimeters) long. Mandarin ducks feed on plants, seeds, insects, snails, and small fish.

 The **red bird of paradise** is about 13 inches (33 centimeters) long. It lives in the rainforest on a few Indonesian islands, where it feeds on fruit, seeds, and insects. Like most birds of paradise, it has colorful plumage and practices a complex courtship ritual.

 The **Carolina anole** can change color from green to brown to match its surroundings. This ability has given it the nickname "American chameleon," though it is not a true chameleon. The anole lives in the southeast United States, and spends much of its time in trees or bushes. It eats spiders, flies, crickets, and other insects. This lizard reaches eight inches (20 centimeters) in length including its long tail.

 The **Indian bullfrog** lives in Southeast Asia, making its home near lakes, rivers, and ponds. This large frog, which measures six and a half inches (16½ centimeters) in length, hunts worms, insects, mice, small birds, snakes, and other frogs.

 The **common milkweed locust** lives in southern Africa. It feeds on the toxic milkweed plant as well as other poisonous plants. These toxins don't affect the locust. Instead, it stores them in its body to use in its own defense. These colorful insects are about two and three-quarters inches (7 centimeters) long.

 The **sarcastic fringehead** is an ambush hunter, lying in wait and grabbing shrimp and small fish when they come close. To protect its territory, it battles other fringeheads in mouth-to-mouth wrestling matches. These fish live in the North American coastal waters of the Pacific Ocean and grow to about eight inches (20 centimeters) in length.

 All **fireflies** are bioluminescent—they produce their own light. *Photuris*, a firefly that uses light as a predatory lure, is found in eastern North America. *Photuris* eats fireflies of other species not just for food, but also to acquire chemicals that repel spiders and other firefly predators. These tricky beetles grow to about half an inch (12 millimeters) in length.

 The **deep-sea dragonfish,** also known as the barbeled dragonfish, is found in all of the world's deep oceans. No plants grow in water that is never reached by sunlight. So, like all deep-sea fish, the dragonfish is a predator, and its needle-sharp teeth ensure that its prey can't escape. Frightening as it looks, the deep-sea dragonfish is only about six inches (15 centimeters) long. It eats the shrimp, squid, and small fish that are attracted to its glowing lure.

 Viewed from above, the **regal ringneck snake** is a solid blue or gray color. It is found in the desert regions of the southwestern United States and northern Mexico. Regal ringnecks eat frogs, lizards, and other snakes. They can reach 33 inches (84 centimeters) in length.

 The **hooded pitohui** eats fruit, seeds, and insects, including the poisonous beetles that provide the toxins found in the pitohui's feathers and skin. This bird also has a crest on its head that it can raise to make itself look larger. The hooded pitohui is about nine inches (23 centimeters) long. It lives in the forests of New Guinea.

 The **ladybird mimic spider** is a kind of orb web spider that lives in China and Japan. It is about one-third inch (8 millimeters) long, and it feeds on small insects that it traps in its web. It is one of several spiders and insects that imitate the toxic ladybird beetle.

The **flag-footed bug** is found throughout the semitropical and tropical regions of the world, where it sucks the juices of plants. In addition to misdirecting the attack of a predator by waving its legs, its unusual feet help camouflage it as it moves about in the leaf litter of the forest floor. This insect's body is about half an inch (12 millimeters) long.

 The body of the **long-tailed widowbird** is about eight inches (20 centimeters) long. The male bird has tail feathers that are twice that length. It flaps its wings slowly, hoping its plumage will catch the eye of a female. When it's not in the air, a male will try to impress a potential mate by spreading its wings and displaying the bright red patch of feathers on its shoulders. These birds live in central and southern Africa and feed on seeds and insects.

 The **stalk-eyed fly** is found in many parts of the world, but it is most common in the tropics of Asia and Africa. It feeds on decaying plants and carrion—dead animals. These curious insects are about one-half inch (12 millimeters) long.

 The **big skate** deserves its name— some of these fish reach almost eight feet (2½ meters) in length. They live on the muddy and sandy sea floors of the coastal Pacific Ocean from Alaska to Mexico. This skate is a bottom feeder, preying on shrimp, crabs, and fish.

 The **bullseye moth** lives in the forests of Central America and northern South America where it sips plant nectar. It has a wingspan of about three inches (7½ centimeters).

When a bullseye moth is startled, it drops to the ground, reveals its eyespots, and twitches violently. This can frighten a bird or other predator.

 The **four-eyed butterflyfish** inhabits the waters of the Caribbean Sea and the western Atlantic Ocean. It eats shrimp, worms, and other small sea creatures. This fish grows to six inches (15 centimeters) in length. Its eyepots can fool an attacker into thinking that the fish's tail is its head. Predators are surprised when the fish escapes by appearing to swim backwards.

 The **ring-tailed lemur** is found only on the island of Madagascar. It is about the size of a house cat, and it feeds on fruit, leaves, and flowers. It also sometimes eats insects and small animals.

For more information

Books:

Animals and Their Colors. By Michael and Patricia Fogden. Crown Publishers, 1974.

Animal Life. By Heidi and Hans-Jürgen Koch. h.f. ullmann, 2008.

Cold Light. By Anita Sitarski. Boyd's Mill Press, 2007.

Dramatic Displays. By Tim Knight. Heinemann Library, 2003.

Extreme Nature. By Mark Carwardine. Harper Collins, 2005.

Feathers. By Robert Clark. Chronicle Books, 2016.

How Animals Live. By Bernard Stonehouse and Esther Bertram. Scholastic Reference, 2004.

How Animals See. By Sandra Sinclair. Facts on File Publications, 1985.

How Animals Work. By David Burnie. Dorling Kindersley, 2010.

Life in the Undergrowth. By David Attenborough. Princeton University Press, 2005.

Steve Backshall's Venom. By Steve Backshall. New Holland, 2007.

Internet:

BBC Nature - Visual Communication.
http://www.bbc.co.uk/nature/adaptations/Visual_perception

Britannica - Display Behaviour.
https://www.britannica.com/topic/display-behaviour

Nature Works - Visual Display.
http://www.nhptv.org/natureworks/nwep3a.htm

Stanford University - Visual Displays.
https://web.stanford.edu/group/stanfordbirds/text/essays/Visual_Displays.html

Useful internet search terms:

animal color

animal display

animal mating display

animal territorial display

animal visual communication

animal visual defenses

animal warning display

For Page —S.J. and R.P.

To learn more about the making of *Look at Me!*
go to **stevejenkins.com/lookatme**